19-
AR 4.2

Baseball's GREATEST STARS

Mike TROUT

by Matt Scheff

SportsZone

An Imprint of Abdo Publishing

abdopublishing.com

Published by Abdo Publishing, a division of ABDO, PO Box 398166, Minneapolis, Minnesota 55439. Copyright © 2016 by Abdo Consulting Group, Inc. International copyrights reserved in all countries. No part of this book may be reproduced in any form without written permission from the publisher. SportsZone™ is a trademark and logo of Abdo Publishing.

Printed in the United States of America, North Mankato, Minnesota
082015
012016

Cover Photos: Chris Carlson/AP Images, foreground; Larry Goren/Four Seam Images/AP Images, background
Interior Photos: Chris Carlson/AP Images, 1 (foreground), 4-5, 6-7; Larry Goren/Four Seam Images/AP Images, 1 (background); Seth Poppel/Yearbook Library, 8-9, 10; Ricardo Arduengo/AP Images, 11, 14-15; Tony Gutierrez/AP Images, 12-13; Jae C. Hong/AP Images, 16; Matt A. Brown/AP Images, 17; Nick Wass/AP Images, 18-19; Cal Sport Media/AP Images, 20-21; Charles Rex Arbogast/AP Images, 22; Kathy Willens/AP Images, 23; Jeff Roberson/AP Images, 24-25; Mark J. Terrill/AP Images, 26-27; Gary Coronado/Houston Chronicle/AP Images, 28-29

Editor: Patrick Donnelly
Series Designer: Laura Polzin

Library of Congress Control Number: 2015946109

Cataloging-in-Publication Data
Scheff, Matt.
 Mike Trout / Matt Scheff.
   p. cm. -- (Baseball's greatest stars)
Includes index.
ISBN 978-1-68078-079-6
1. Trout, Mike, 1991- --Juvenile literature. 2. Baseball players--United States--Biography--Juvenile literature.   I. Title.
796.357092--dc23
[B]   2015946109

CONTENTS

WALKING OFF

The Los Angeles Angels were in a tough spot on May 15, 2014. They trailed the Tampa Bay Rays 5-2 in the bottom of the ninth inning. Then the Angels started a rally. The first two batters walked. Outfielder Collin Cowgill stroked a single to drive in a run. The Rays' lead was down to two runs.

More than 30,000 Angels fans were on their feet. Next up was baseball's best hitter, 22-year-old Mike Trout.

Mike Trout celebrates after coming through for the Angels.

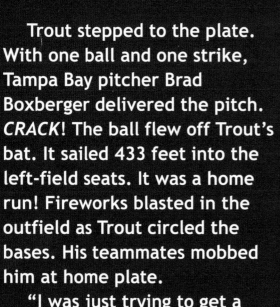

Trout stepped to the plate. With one ball and one strike, Tampa Bay pitcher Brad Boxberger delivered the pitch. *CRACK*! The ball flew off Trout's bat. It sailed 433 feet into the left-field seats. It was a home run! Fireworks blasted in the outfield as Trout circled the bases. His teammates mobbed him at home plate.

"I was just trying to get a base hit," Trout explained after the game. "It's an unbelievable feeling."

Trout receives a warm welcome from his teammates after his home run beat the Rays.

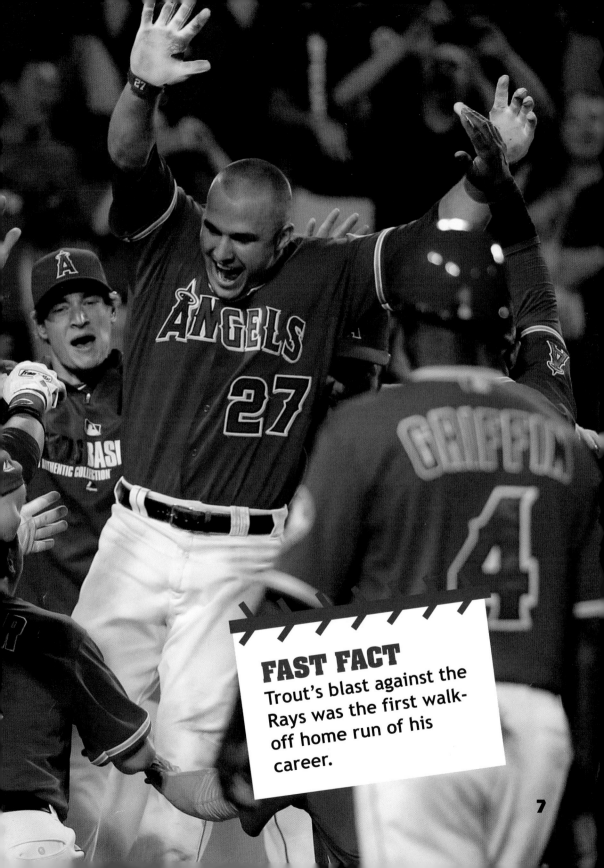

FAST FACT

Trout's blast against the Rays was the first walk-off home run of his career.

EARLY LIFE

Michael Nelson Trout was born on August 7, 1991, in Vineland, New Jersey. Mike's father, Jeff, had been a baseball player in the minor leagues. But a knee injury led him to retire before he ever reached the big leagues.

Jeff went on to become a coach at Millville High School in New Jersey. His son was often by his side.

Mike, *center*, also played basketball at Millville High School.

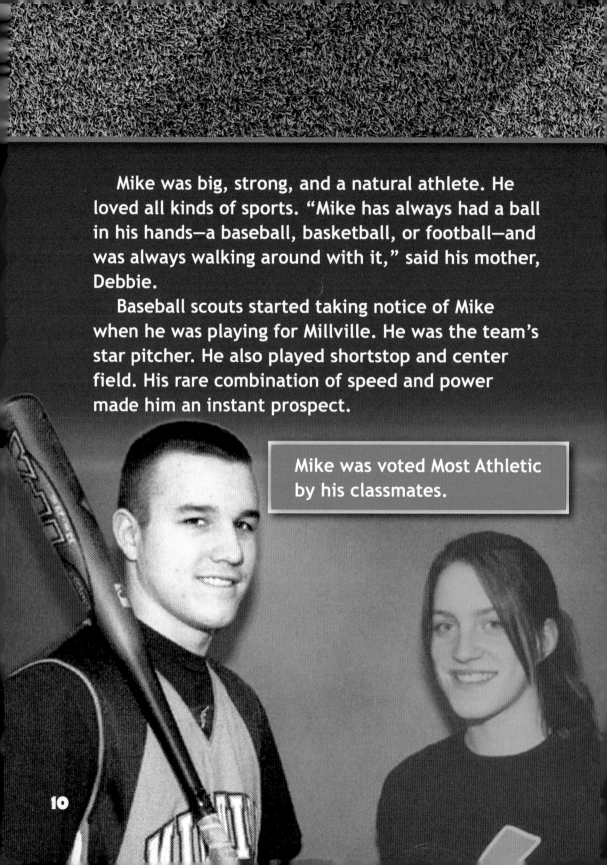

Mike was big, strong, and a natural athlete. He loved all kinds of sports. "Mike has always had a ball in his hands—a baseball, basketball, or football—and was always walking around with it," said his mother, Debbie.

Baseball scouts started taking notice of Mike when he was playing for Millville. He was the team's star pitcher. He also played shortstop and center field. His rare combination of speed and power made him an instant prospect.

Mike was voted Most Athletic by his classmates.

Mike always played hard and did not mind if his uniform got dirty.

FAST FACT
Mike's favorite baseball player was Derek Jeter. He even wore No. 2 on his jersey—just like Jeter—when he was a child.

Millville advanced to the state playoffs when Mike was a junior. The other teams knew he was a dangerous hitter. Opposing pitchers often intentionally walked Mike. One team even did so when the bases were loaded.

Mike belted 18 home runs as a senior in 2009. It was a New Jersey high school record. He accepted a scholarship offer to play baseball at East Carolina University. But pro ball would soon be calling.

Mike got a lot of chances to practice his big-league home run trot when he was in high school.

SUPER PROSPECT

Major League Baseball (MLB) invited several players to its draft in 2009. Trout was the only one who showed up. TV cameras showed him watching and waiting. Pick after pick passed. Finally, the Angels selected him with pick 25 of the first round.

Trout reported to the Angels' rookie-league team in Arizona for his first minor league season. He was a hitting machine. Trout started to rocket up the minor league ranks.

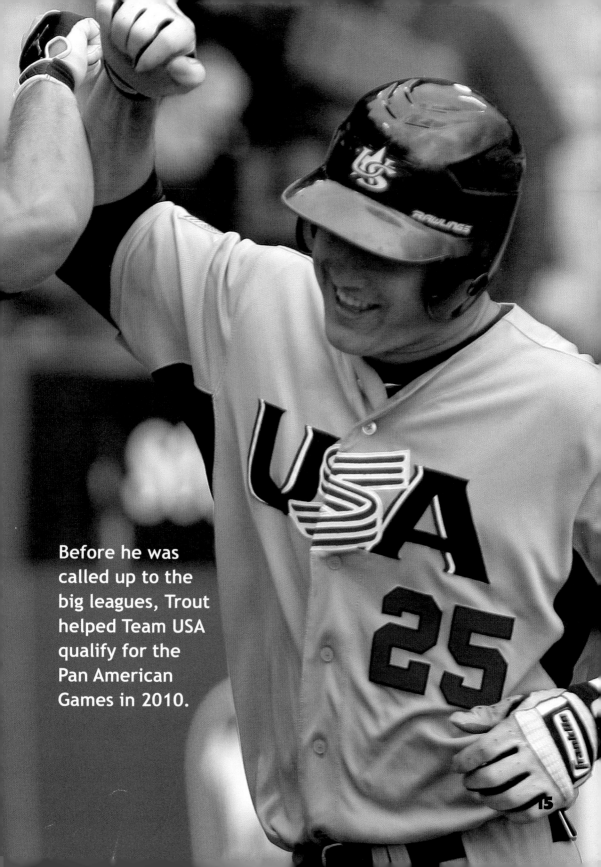

Before he was called up to the big leagues, Trout helped Team USA qualify for the Pan American Games in 2010.

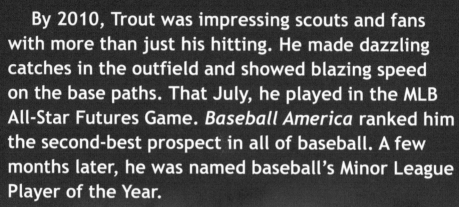

By 2010, Trout was impressing scouts and fans with more than just his hitting. He made dazzling catches in the outfield and showed blazing speed on the base paths. That July, he played in the MLB All-Star Futures Game. *Baseball America* ranked him the second-best prospect in all of baseball. A few months later, he was named baseball's Minor League Player of the Year.

Trout started the 2011 season in the minors. But the Angels could not keep him down for long.

Trout, *left*, represented the United States in the 2010 MLB All-Star Futures Game.

Before the 2011 season was over, Trout had made his major league debut.

FAST FACT
At 19 years, 2 months old, Trout became the youngest player ever to be named Minor League Player of the Year.

BIG LEAGUER

The Angels finally called up their young star on July 8, 2011. Trout got his first hit a night later. His first home run came on July 24. Still, the 20-year-old struggled at times. He split the rest of the season between the minors and the majors. He batted just .220 in 40 big-league games.

Teammates greet Trout at home plate after he hit his first major league home run in a game at Baltimore.

Trout again started in the minors in 2012. On April 28, the Angels called him back up. This time, he was there to stay. He took the league by storm, getting hit after hit and making amazing catches in the outfield. He batted .326 for the season. He led the league with 49 stolen bases and 129 runs. He was named the American League (AL) Rookie of the Year. He also finished second in Most Valuable Player (MVP) voting.

Trout takes a cut against the Los Angeles Dodgers during his rookie season.

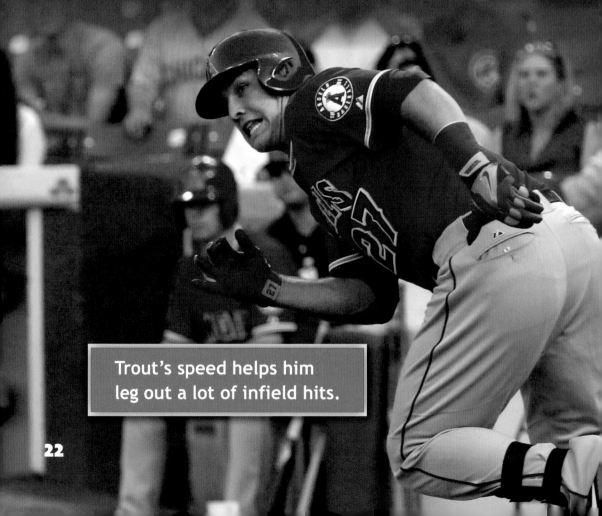

By 2013, Trout was one of baseball's biggest stars. He started for the AL in the All-Star Game in July. Trout seemed to be hitting everything. Yet the Angels struggled. They started poorly and never recovered. Trout might have had the best season of any player that year. But he again finished second in MVP voting.

Trout's speed helps him leg out a lot of infield hits.

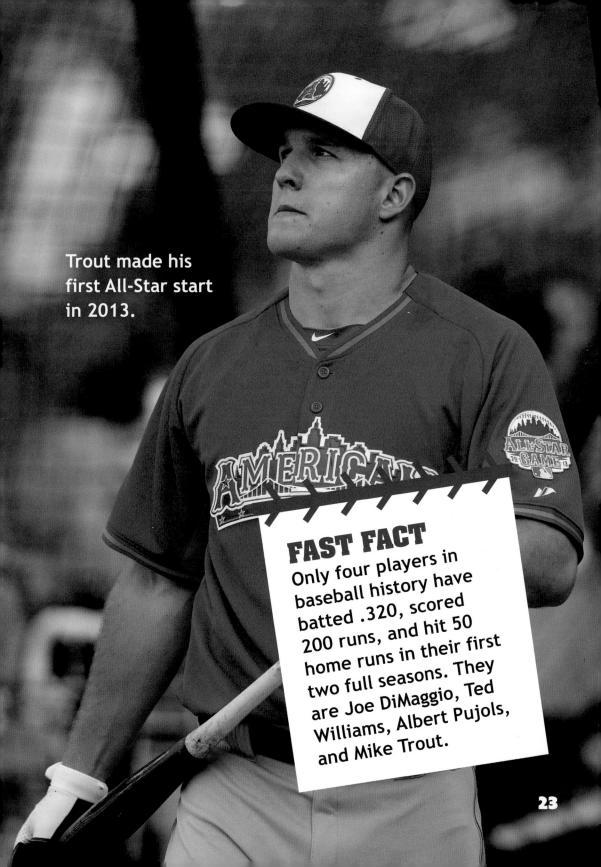

Trout made his first All-Star start in 2013.

FAST FACT

Only four players in baseball history have batted .320, scored 200 runs, and hit 50 home runs in their first two full seasons. They are Joe DiMaggio, Ted Williams, Albert Pujols, and Mike Trout.

MOST VALUABLE ANGEL

Before the 2014 season, the Angels rewarded Trout. They signed him to a new six-year contract. It was worth $144.5 million.

Trout got to work earning that money. He started the season red-hot and just kept hitting. In July, he was named MVP of the All-Star Game. Then Trout led a late-season surge that helped the Angels win the AL West Division. He was rewarded with his first AL MVP Award.

Trout got to play with his boyhood idol, Derek Jeter, at the 2014 All-Star Game.

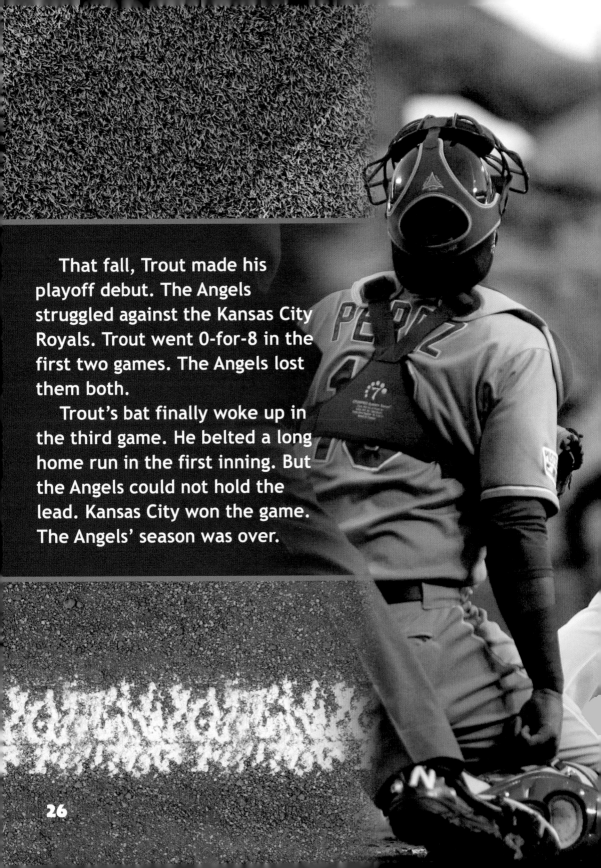

That fall, Trout made his playoff debut. The Angels struggled against the Kansas City Royals. Trout went 0-for-8 in the first two games. The Angels lost them both.

Trout's bat finally woke up in the third game. He belted a long home run in the first inning. But the Angels could not hold the lead. Kansas City won the game. The Angels' season was over.

Trout and the Angels made it to the playoffs in 2014 but were frustrated in losing to the Royals.

Few players in baseball history have had as much early success as Trout. His play has earned comparisons to legends such as Willie Mays and Mickey Mantle. He is a rare "five-tool" player. That means he hits for average and power, runs well, plays great defense, and has a strong throwing arm.

Can Trout keep up this pace? If so, he may go down as one of the greatest players in history.

Trout, *right*, and his teammates celebrate another Angels victory.

TIMELINE

1991
Michael Nelson Trout is born on August 7 in Vineland, New Jersey.

2009
Trout belts 18 home runs as a high school senior. The Angels draft him. He begins his pro career in the minor leagues.

2010
Trout is named baseball's Minor League Player of the Year.

2011
Trout makes his major league debut on July 8. He hits his first home run on July 24.

2012
Trout wins the AL Rookie of the Year Award and finishes second in AL MVP voting.

2013
Trout makes the AL All-Star team and again finishes second in AL MVP voting.

2014
Trout wins the AL MVP award and leads the Angels to the playoffs.

2015
Trout becomes the youngest player in baseball history to reach 100 career home runs and stolen bases.

GLOSSARY

DEBUT
First appearance.

PROSPECT
An athlete likely to succeed at the next level.

RALLY
A series of walks and hits that result in multiple runs.

ROOKIE
A first-year player.

SCHOLARSHIP
Money given to a student to pay for education expenses.

SCOUT
A person who evaluates talent and reports back to his or her employer.

WALK-OFF HOME RUN
A home run that puts the home team ahead in the final inning, forcing the visiting team's players to walk off the field.

INDEX

ABOUT THE AUTHOR

Matt Scheff is an artist and author living in Alaska. He enjoys mountain climbing, deep-sea fishing, and curling up with his two Siberian huskies to watch baseball.